# WHERE GOOD MEANS THE BEST

# Where GOOD Means the BEST

## 70 YEARS AT FRANK'S BAKE SHOP

by
**Brian F. Swartz**

## Maine Origins Publications
### An imprint of Epic Saga Publishing
### Brewer, Maine, USA

# WHERE GOOD MEANS THE BEST:
## 70 YEARS AT FRANK'S BAKE SHOP

### PHOTOS

Photos from Chapter 9 are courtesy of the Bangor Daily News. Photographers are Kevin Bennett, Bridget Brown, Gabor Degre, Denise Farwell, Linda Coan O'Kresik, Megan Rathfon, and John Clarke Russ.

Some photos are courtesy of Brian F. Swartz.

Photo of Franklin Delano Roosevelt at Campobello Island from the National Archives and Records Administration, ARC Identifier 196819.

Author photo of Brian F. Swartz is by Gabor Degre.

All other photos are courtesy of Frank's Bake Shop, the Soucy family, and Chris Pierson.

### SPECIAL THANKS

The Soucy family would like to thank Irv Marsters and Richard R. Shaw for their excellent suggestion that made possible this commemorative book celebrating the 70th anniversary of Frank's Bake Shop.

The publisher would like to thank the Bangor Daily News for allowing the use of its photos.

ISBN: 978-0-9833346-4-4

Published by Maine Origins Publications
An imprint of Epic Saga Publishing
Brewer, Maine USA

# Dedication from the Soucy Family

*We would like to dedicate this book to*

*Grammy & Grampy,*
*Mom & Dad,*
*and Uncle Frank & Aunt Mary*

*...and to the hundreds of employees*
*who have made Frank's*
*"Where GOOD means the BEST."*

# Contents

# Introduction

# Where Good
# Means the Best

The Soucys acquired the building adjacent to the bakery on State Street some years after Frank's Bake Shop opened. As kids, we called the building "Mrs. Bell's."

We developed a small catering hall, known as the East Room, with a full kitchen in the basement that accommodated about 60 people. The hall was great for business meetings, luncheons, small parties, and our family gatherings, as our families increased in size.

After Dad passed away, we knew as a family that the building we called "home" — at 199 State Street — needed major work done to it. We either had to sell the property "as is" or go all out and build a business that our father would be proud of.

We could not imagine Bangor without a Frank's Bake Shop, so we decided to update our "home."

We also knew that it would be a major undertaking. Theresa was the general manager of the bakery at the time, Bernadette the assistant manager, and Dick took care of repairs and maintenance.

Over the years, Dick had taken on many remodeling projects on our property, such as renovating the East Room. So when we updated the bakery, Dick took on the duties of a general contractor, hiring the architects and subcontractors and working alongside them to complete the modernization — all with the monumental task of not

Standing before a portrait of their parents Walteen and Joe Soucy are (from left) Joe, Fleurette, Theresa, Bernadette, and Dick.

closing the bakery for even a single day.

Looking back to 1945, as a family we endured the hardships and costs to put together not just a building, but a building that has served the greater Bangor area for 70 years. Dad had always said it would be nice to have retail space where customers could come into the shop, sit down, and enjoy their morning pastries and coffee with other folks.

One of our goals was to make that dream a reality.

Dad built his business with his dad, Frank, and brother, Frank Jr., and with love. Everyone loved Joe and Walteen and enjoyed having them around at all the catering functions put on by the bakery.

Even though our project is still not fully complete today, it is done with the love and care passed on from our father.

The hundreds of employees whom we were blessed to have working with us at the bakery over the years became family, and we could not have grown without them.

Frank's Bake Shop became not just a building, but a Bangor institution, and our hope is that it will continue to be such for years to come.

Thank you for sharing the last 70 years with the Soucy family!

Joe Soucy
Fleurette Soucy Dow
Theresa Soucy
Bernadette Soucy Gaspar
Dick Soucy

On August 15, 1925, a professional photographer captured a smiling employee standing at the entrance to the A&P store located at 199 State Street, Bangor. Purchased by the Soucy family in 1947, this store became the new home of Frank's Bake Shop that year.

# Chapter 1

# Frank's Bake Shop: The Early Years

**B**orn in St. Hubert in Quebec Province in Canada in 1883, Ferdinand "Frank" J. Soucy learned the art of cooking at a young age. Children often worked on a family farm in that era; Frank found employment elsewhere as his father, a lumberjack, traveled each fall to logging camps deep in the Quebec forests.

Frank went with him. Everyone living at a logging camp was expected to pull his weight; although too small to help the lumberjacks harvest trees, Frank was the right size to assist the camp cook, who prepared meals for hungry loggers.

So Frank learned how to cook breakfasts, dinners, and desserts on wood stoves. During the 1890s, his cooking skills took him to logging camps farther afield in Quebec and then across the border to Maine, where he worked at camps in the forests drained by the Penobscot River.

Arriving in Bangor in the early 20th century, Frank settled down on the East Side. He married Mary Veilleux in a 1907 ceremony at St. John's Catholic Church on York Street. Frank worked as a baker for other businesses in the Queen City area for the next 41 years.

The Soucys had 12 children: Jeannette, Dorothy, Genevieve, Edith, Mary, Robert, Henry, Joseph, John, Frank Jr., Don, and James.

Joseph (known as "Joe") was born on May 4, 1917. The Army drafted Joe during World War II, but he contracted rheumatic fever during his basic training at an Army post in the South; given a medical discharge, he shipped home to Bangor and later worked as a mail sorter on the daily Maine Central Railroad train between Bangor and Brunswick.

Born in Brewer on December 4, 1925, Frank Jr. graduated from John Bapst Memorial High School in 1944 and then became a bookkeeper at Dow Field in Bangor.

In 1945, Frank Soucy Sr. was the head baker at the University of Maine, but he decided to start his own bakery. Joe saw no future as a mail sorter, and Frank Jr. sought a new challenge. Putting their cash together and coming up with $200, the Soucys opened Frank's Bake

Around 1910, Mary Veilleux Soucy and Ferdinand "Frank" Soucy (rear) attended the wedding of Joseph Stanley Poulin and Lea Alexandrine Soucy Poulin (front). Lea and Frank were siblings, as were Mary Soucy and Joseph Poulin. Frank, who worked as a baker in Bangor, had arranged the wedding for Lea; she specifically moved to Bangor to marry Joseph.

A typical work day at Frank's Bake Shop in the late 1940s finds (from left) Frank Soucy Sr., Ray Jewell, Joseph A. Soucy, and Dwight Fraser preparing hot dogs. Some employees arrived in the wee hours of the morning to begin baking the day's breads and pastries for customers who would arrive when the store opened at 9 a.m.

Shop at 148 Hancock Street in Bangor.

In ledger entries dated October 17, 1945, Joe Soucy listed some equipment that the Soucys had acquired for their new business, which officially opened to the public that November 17. The Soucys offered baked beans, breads, and such pastries as brownies, cookies, cream rolls, Danishes, and many kinds of doughnuts.

Aunt Doris Soucy thought up the bakery's motto, "Where Good Means the Best."

Meanwhile, an A&P store was located in leased space at 199 State Street, a block from St. John's Catholic Church. The building's owner fielded countless phone calls about maintenance issues; fed up with the constant problems with his property, he told his tailor, "I'd sell it in a minute" for a $1,000 down payment.

The tailor shared that news with his friend, Joe Soucy, who spoke with his father and brother about buying 199 State Street to gain more space and greater visibility for their bakery. All three Soucys concurred; Frank's Bake Shop moved to the new location in 1947.

Settling down on the East Side of Bangor after their 1907 wedding, Ferdinand "Frank" Soucy and his wife, Mary, had 12 children. After working as a baker for many years, Frank Sr. decided to open his own bakery in 1945. He discussed his plans with sons Joseph and Frank Jr., who were working at other jobs that left them dissatisfied. Joe and Frank supported their father's plans to open Frank's Bake Shop; located in leased space at 148 Hancock Street, Bangor, the bakery started on October 17, 1945. Frank's Bake Shop moved to 199 State Street, Bangor in 1947.

**Above:** In the late 1940s, Joseph A. Soucy (right) and Ray Jewell bake Vienna bread in an oven at Frank's Bake Shop, 199 State Street, Bangor. As Joe pulls the bread loaves from the oven, Ray glazes them with butter.

**Below:** By the late 1940s, baked goods sold by Frank's Bake Shop were in such demand that the Soucy family made deliveries in Bangor. Making a delivery run somewhere in the Queen City, the bakery's International rolls along a Bangor street.

**Above:** Circa Easter 1948, the staff at Frank's Bake Shop prepared many types of cakes for customers to buy. Frank's Bake Shop and other bakeries belonged to Pine Tree Associates, an alliance that let its members combine their "buying power," according to Bernadette Soucy Gaspar. Baking supplies shipped by rail to a Veazie warehouse, where each Pine Tree Associates member picked up its desired stock.

**Below:** Among the many Easter-related baked items on sale at Frank's Bake Shop circa 1949 were the Specialty Cakes.

**Above:** Waiting to greet customers at Frank's Bake Shop circa Easter 1948 are (from left) Frank Soucy Jr., Joe Soucy, Norma Dubay, Genevieve Twitchell (an aunt of the Soucys), Mary Soucy (also an aunt), and Dwight Fraser.

**Below:** On April 28, 1943, Joseph Soucy married Walteen Gagnier, an Aroostook County native who had moved to Bangor in 1932. She worked as a housekeeper in Bangor until her marriage to Joe. Frank Soucy Sr. baked and decorated this wedding cake for the reception held for his son and new daughter-in-law.

The hard-working Walteen did more than clean house for her clients. According to her daughter, Bernadette Soucy Gaspar, a Bangor woman came home from work to find her house spotless and a delicious meal prepared for the family. The woman asked her housekeeper, Walteen, who had done the cooking; learning that Walteen had served up a delicious supper and cleaned the house from top to bottom, the woman could not believe that one person could do so much work in one day. Joe and Walteen and their children (Joseph, Richard, Bernadette, Theresa, and Fleurette) lived beside Frank's Bake Shop at 199 State Street, Bangor.

**Above:**
Joe Soucy rings up a purchase made by an unidentified customer at Frank's Bake Shop at 199 State Street, Bangor, circa 1949. The employee watching Joe at work is Elizabeth "Libby" Campbell.

**Left:**
A Thanksgiving window display in the late 1940s advertises the various holiday-related foods available at the bakery. Joey Soucy remembers that a particular Thanksgiving season saw a live turkey displayed in the bakery window.

**Top:**
This is the ledger from the first day that Joseph Soucy opened Frank's Bake Shop on October 17, 1945. Including $200 he, his brother, and his father pooled together, the trio launched their business with just $1,400.

**Above:**
This is the first handwritten entry in Joe's ledger: "I, Joseph A. Soucy, have opened a bakery at 148 Hancock Street in the name of Frank's Bakery with the following assets and liabilities..."

**Above:** Joe Soucy loads a cake pan into a 16-pan Johnson's Deck Oven installed at Frank's Bake Shop in the late 1940s. Heated with oil and equipped with a gun-type oil burner, the oven came with a 275-gallon oil tank. The price for the oven and oil tank was $650.00. **Facing page:** An advertisement in the Bangor Daily News announced the relocation of Frank's Bake Shop from 148 Hancock St., Bangor to a new location at 199 State St., Bangor, circa November 1, 1947. To place an order by telephone, customers dialed 6710. Below is a closer look at the main text of the advertisement.

In order to meet the increased demands for our bakery products, we have moved from 148 Hancock Street to a new location at 199 State Street. Our new location provides ample room for expansion and for an increased and improved service.

Since November 14, 1945 when we first opened our bakery, we have constantly enlarged our facilities to keep up with our trade. We have always insisted on maintaining a high standard of quality in all our bakery products. Our business has been built on this fact plus a policy of fair dealing and service.

We will be pleased to meet all our old patrons at our new location and we invite the public to visit us on our open house to inspect our modern, spotless, efficient bakery. Watch for our open house announcement!

A baker named Vivian decorates a loaf cake with chocolate frosting at Frank's Bake Shop circa 1950.

# Chapter 2

# The 1950s: A Time of Growth

When Frank Soucy Sr. and his sons Frank Jr. and Joe relocated Frank's Bake Shop to 199 State Street, Bangor in autumn 1947, they were not sure how well the new business would do.

Customers quickly let them know. The bakery sold out that first day, and the Soucys posted $67 in sales to their business's ledger. Bread sold for 25 cents a loaf, and cookies and doughnuts for about 40 cents a dozen.

The Soucys advertised their "Fresh-From-The-Oven Favorites" in the local newspapers. Mouths watered as customers scanned the list: apple and raspberry turnovers, chocolate fudge and orange cakes, cream rolls and chocolate éclairs and napoleons, doughnuts, cream pies (chocolate, lemon, and vanilla cream), and "plain pies" (apple, blueberry, custard, and squash). Frank's Bake Shop also served "Delicious Oven Baked Beans," and customers could place their orders by dialing 6710.

The bakery's new location was perfect for attracting local and out-of-town customers. "The main road north and south [in Bangor] was State Street," explained Bernadette Soucy Gaspar. "There was no interstate highway until the '60s," so people coming in Bangor from points north or south drove right past Frank's

A well-known photograph taken of Frank's Bake Shop circa 1950 shows the popular Bangor bakery lit up after dark. The bakery had not yet expanded to occupy the full front of 199 State Street as the business does today.

Bake Shop.

The Soucys introduced new products and services. A really big hit was hard-serve ice cream, which Joe Soucy made in the front of the bakery. "We made about 39 flavors," Bernadette recalled. "Many people walked the streets on a hot summer's eve and stopped by for ice cream.

The shop was usually open until 9 p.m.. "Sometimes we did not close until 10 p.m. because people were waiting."

When parents started telling Joe that their children really enjoyed soft-serve ice cream, he introduced that treat, too.

Bernadette said that Frank's Bake Shop was the first on State

Street to make pizza. "Brother Joey and cousin Don McCann would work all night to make pre-baked 12-inch shells, which were frozen for later use," she recalled. "We could bake two pizzas at a time in our little pizza oven at 450-500 degrees."

Dwight Fraser was the first baker hired who was unrelated to the Soucys. He was soon joined in the early 1950s by Walter Beaulieu (another baker) and Ben Gunn, who handled deliveries.

Frank's Bake Service started offering off-site catering in the late 1950s. "Dad mostly took care of the catering and the bakery, and Uncle Frank [Soucy Jr.] did most of the cake decorating," Bernadette said. "Both crossed over to help each other when needed."

The bakery catered many wedding receptions (often two or

The Soucy family made extensive renovations to the showroom of Frank's Bake Shop in 1953; later, they added a take-out window, seen in this photo from around 1961. The bakery had introduced Frank's Ice Cream just a few years earlier; customers could walk up to a service window on Brown Street and order a single scoop of ice cream in a cone for 15 cents.

three per weekend) by serving finger foods on silver and glass serving dishes. "If we did large sit-down meals such as the Masons, Shriners, or Airstream Trailers, and there was coffee left over, Mom would make coffee Jell-O," she said.

During the 1950s, the Soucys opened the Annex in Bangor. Located on Hammond Street, the Annex sold goods from Frank's Bake Shop. Three Soucy brothers—Joe, Frank Jr., and Don—worked there, as did Ben Gunn. The Soucys sold the Annex to Ben Goodstein in the mid-1960s.

**Above:** In the early 1950s, a delivery vehicle belonging to Frank's Bake Shop Inc. is parked outside the bakery at 199 State St., Bangor. The service station across the street was located on the current site of the parking lot for Miller Drug.

**Facing page top:** Joe Soucy displays the fruit cakes made at Frank's Bake Shop for one Christmas sometime in the mid-1950s.

**Facing page bottom:** Fruit cakes were popular at Christmas in the mid-1950s, and Frank's Bake Shop in Bangor baked many for the holiday season.

**Above:**
With Frank's Bake Shop decorated for Easter and the display cases filled with the appropriate baked items, Elenor Verow awaits customers sometime in the mid-1950s.

**Facing page top:**
Sometime in the 1950s, Joe Soucy stands in the Doughnut Room in front of the fryolators used to make doughnuts at Frank's Bake Shop in Bangor.

**Facing page bottom:**
Prepared in fryolators in the Doughnut Room at Frank's Bake Shop in Bangor, doughnuts were glazed and then placed on dowels inserted into a wall board. The warm glazing dripped until it hardened, and the drippings were collected in metal pans.

Walteen and Joe Soucy cater a wedding reception in Bangor in the late 1950s, a few years after Frank's Bake Shop started catering off-site events in Bangor and elsewhere. "I can envision Mom and Dad running into the house to clean up after prepping in the bakery," recalled Bernadette. "Mom painted her red nails, and Dad put on his very starched white shirt and cuff links."

Walteen Soucy (left) caters a wedding reception in the Bangor area in the late 1950s.

**Above:** When a meal needed to be served to a large number of people gathering at the new Bangor Auditorium for a special event in the late 1950s, Frank's Bake Shop was hired to cater the meal. The auditorium, capable of seating almost 6,000 people, opened on October 1, 1955.

**Below:** In the 1960s, Frank's Bake Shop occupied the left side of 199 State Street in Bangor, and Joe and Walteen Soucy lived with their family on the right side of the wood-framed building.

Bangor Daily News photo by John Clarke Russ

Since Frank's Bake Shop opened on October 17, 1945, its bakers have created exquisitely decorated Christmas cookies that are eagerly sought by customers.

Gathered outside Frank's Bake Shop at 199 State Street, Bangor in summer 1951 are four of the children of Joe and Walteen Soucy. Front, from left, are Bernadette and Theresa; rear, from left, are Joey and Dick.

# Chapter 3

# Growing Up
# At Frank's

**W**hen Frank Soucy Sr. and his sons Frank Jr. and Joe relocated Frank's Bake Shop to 199 State Street, Bangor in autumn 1947, they were not sure how well the new business would do.

For the five children of Joe and Walteen Soucy, growing up at Frank's Bake Shop came naturally; the family lived beside the bakery at 199 State Street in Bangor. The entrance to their home was located where the bakery's entrance is today.

Joey was born in 1944, Dick in 1945, Bernadette in 1947, Theresa in 1949, and Fleurette in 1950. Because four of their birthdays fell between June 25th and July 24th Walteen Soucy would organize a big birthday party that often saw many children attending to celebrate all four birthdays. Instead of baking a cake in later years, Walteen would make strawberry pie "with lots of cream poured into it," Bernadette said.

"We had jobs [in the bakery] as young as five years old, making boxes," she recalled; they were paid one penny per five boxes. A nearby destination where the children spent their "pay" was Flemming's Market on York Street, where candy was two pieces for a penny.

For the Soucys, a childhood spent growing up at Frank's often

Joe and Walteen Soucy are the proud parents of son Dick Soucy after his first communion was observed at St. John's Catholic Church in Bangor in 1951. Taken outside Frank's Bake Shop at 199 State Street, Bangor, this photograph also shows the bakery's International delivery vehicle; through the 1950s, Frank's Bake Shop delivered baked goods to such locations as the Bangor State Hospital, Dow Air Force Base, the University of Maine, Eastern Maine General Hospital, and downtown restaurants.

focused on the bakery. Children often delivered May baskets to other children in the mid-1950s; the Soucys did, too, and Walteen saw a business opportunity. For many years she traveled to Ellsworth and picked up May baskets from a church group to sell in the bakery.

"We now sell about 400 every year," Bernadette said.

Joe and Walteen Soucy had an open charge account at a pharmacy next door that was owned by Bill Houlihan. The children, who liked Aspergum, would get some at the pharmacy and place the purchases on their parents' account. This continued until Walteen read the statement from Houlihan!

Bernadette's earliest memory of the bakery was sitting in the office on her father's lap when she was three years old. Later, grandfather Frank Sr. would let her sit next to him on a high stool with a red seat, and give her a small rolling pin and a piece of dough and let her roll it.

When a dog came into the family's life, the children argued about a name. Walteen finally settled the disagreement by saying, "We'll just call him 'Pierre.'"

Gathered in the Soucy family home for a photograph in January 1956 are (front, from left) sisters Bernadette Soucy, Fleurette Soucy, and Theresa Soucy; (rear, from left) cousin Linda Saucier and brothers Joey Soucy and Dick Soucy.

In 1956, Theresa Soucy (left) observed her first communion, and her sister, Bernadette, observed her confirmation at St. John's Catholic Church in Bangor. This photograph was taken outside Frank's Bake Shop; note the elm trees growing on both sides of the street in that era.

He became a fixture with the Soucy family and at the bakery. Before there was ever a sign saying, "No dogs allowed," Pierre would walk into the bakery and stand in front of the cookie case until the employee at the counter gave him a sugar cookie (Pierre's favorite). On warm summer days Pierre would lay down by the air conditioner and stay cool. He was one smart dog!

The Soucys attended St. John's Catholic School on State Street. Afterward, the boys attended John Bapst Memorial High School on Broadway, and the girls went to the Academy of St. Joseph, a boarding school in South Berwick.

The five Soucys all worked in the bakery while growing up. Joey worked as a baker and made deliveries; Dick made ice cream and did painting and carpentry behind the scenes; and Bernadette, Theresa, and Fleurette worked up front and helped their parents with catering. Bernadette and Theresa work there full time today.

Dick, who has taught for many years at John Bapst, still does repairs and handles building projects at the bakery.

Joey and Dick wielded snow shovels to clean snow off the sidewalk outside the bakery in winter, and Walteen often tugged a hose across that same sidewalk in summer to spray State Street and keep down the dust outside the bakery's front door.

"People passing by would say, 'Hey, Walteen, I didn't know you worked for the city!" Bernadette said.

One Sunday in May 1957, the children of Joe and Walteen Soucy dressed up for church and for dinner at the Oronoka Restaurant in Orono. Sporting the latest in spring fashions are (front, from left) Theresa and Fleurette and (rear, from left) Bernadette, Dick, and Joey.

**Above:**
Dressed up for Easter Sunday in the early 1960s are (from left) Joe Soucy, Fleurette Soucy, Bernadette Soucy, Theresa Soucy, and Walteen Soucy. The family poses in front of Frank's Bake Shop at 199 State Street, Bangor.

**Facing page:**
Theresa Soucy poses on the sidewalk in front of Frank's Bake Shop at 199 State St., Bangor circa 1957. Behind her is a café inside a building now owned by the Soucy family and operated as Healthy Solutions.

**Above:** Joe Soucy caters a reception held at a downtown Bangor bank sometime during the 1960s.

**Below:** The children of Joe and Walteen Soucy grew up working at Frank's Bake Shop. Here, oldest brother Joey works in a food-preparation area sometime during the 1960s.

**Above:** Walteen and Joseph Soucy share a kiss while celebrating their 40th wedding anniversary in April 1983. Their children organized a surprise party for the occasion.

**Below:** The Soucy family poses for a photograph in 1983 during the 40th anniversary of the wedding of Joseph and Walteen Soucy. Joining for the photograph are (from left) Theresa Soucy, Joey Soucy, Fleurette Dow, Joseph Soucy, Walteen Soucy, Bernadette Soucy Gaspar, and Richard "Dick" Soucy.

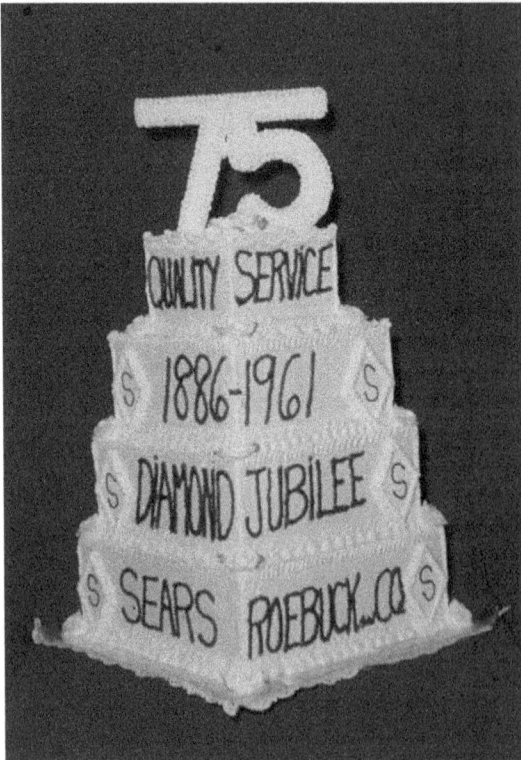

**Above:** In July 1985, Walteen Soucy steps one last time from her beloved Cadillac, which she had purchased from Mrs. Boyle, the woman whom Walteen cared for before she married Joe Soucy. The Cadillac bore the Maine license plate 555. Despite efforts made by a non-family member to acquire that plate number, Walteen kept it; daughter Theresa Soucy has this same license-plate number today.

**Left:** In 1961, Frank's Bake Shop baked this cake for the Sears & Roebuck store in downtown Bangor upon the 75th anniversary of Sears & Roebuck.

**Left:**
Bernadette and Walteen Soucy are greeted by Pierre, the spitz-collie mix who charmed many customers of Frank's Bakery.

When the Soucys acquired the dog, "We were arguing about a name" for it, recalled Bernadette. "Mom said, "We'll just call him 'Pierre.'"

**Below:** On a pleasant day in the 1960s, Pierre receives the adulation of his Soucy fans, including Walteen (seated) and (from left) Mary Kelly, Dominic Soucy, Joe Soucy, and Margaret Kelly. The Kellys and Dominic Soucy were, respectively, nieces and a nephew of Joe and Walteen Soucy.

By July 1961, Frank's Bake Shop had added Cree-Mee ice cream. "Customers told Dad, 'We like coming to Frank's for ice cream, but our kids want the dairy cream,' so we put in a machine to make everyone happy," recalls Bernadette. Around the corner on Brown Street was a service window where customers could step up and order ice cream cones.

# Chapter 4

# The 1960s:
# The Best Prime
# Rib in the World

O n Thursday, July 13, 1961, Joe and Frank Soucy celebrated the fifteenth anniversary of Frank's Bake Shop after extensively remodeling "its retail store," according to an article published in the Bangor Daily News.

While the actual fifteenth anniversary had occurred the previous October, remodeling had delayed the official observance nine months. Although the facilities had undergone quite a change, the quality food and service for which the bakery was known had not.

According to Joe Soucy, doughnuts remained the top seller with customers; Frank's fried 6,000 of them daily. The Soucys "make their own jellies, jams, pickles and piccalilli," the BDN stated. "In addition, they make their own Italian meat balls and sauce and can prepare a feast of chicken or roast beef for as many as 500 people."

"It's a real smorgasbord," Joe Soucy told the BDN at the time, referring to the bakery's diversified cuisine. "And we have served a smorgasbord for as many as 500 people."

The previous summer, Frank's Bake Shop had garnered local fame by providing catering services for the filming of the Hollywood film *Sunrise at Campobello* on Campobello Island in New Brunswick.

Bangor Daily News, Wednesday, July 12, 1961    9

from Our
Newly Remodeled, Sparkling Fresh Shop

*Grand* **REOPENING** Thursday July 13

## OUR 15th ANNIVERSARY and REOPENING SPECIALS
### THURSDAY, FRIDAY, SATURDAY

Cherry Walnut
**Anniversary Cake** **75¢**
It's our anniversary . . . You get the Cake at 50¢ off the regular price.

OUR OWN **ICE CREAM** ½ Gal. Reg. $1.25 **99¢** Pt. Reg. 38¢ **28¢**

COOKIES Butter Crunch Chocolate Chip Spanish Walnut Peanut Salted USUALLY 49¢ **35¢** Doz. CHICKEN PIE REG. $1.15 **95¢** EA.

OUR OWN ITALIAN STYLE

DONUTS Chocolate Krysted Plain, Jelly Water Iced USUALLY 60¢ **50¢** Doz. **Meat Balls and Sauce** USUALLY 88¢ **65¢** PT.

REGISTER FOR BAKED STUFFED TURKEY
and other prizes to be given away. No obligation to buy . . . just come in.

COME IN TOMORROW AND MEET
MR. JOHN RECHIS
Bakery Consultant, WESSON OIL CO.

John Rechis is known as one of the nation's top bakery specialists, having held demonstrations for commercial bakers all over the world. His talents come from 25 years of experience starting as a pan greaser and working up to master baker extraordinary.

While at Frank's Bake Shop Mr. Rechis will bake and serve New York Style Cheese Cake as well as a variety of cookies.

COME IN . . . MEET MR. RECHIS THURSDAY
FROM 1 P.M. TO 6 P.M.

The following firms take pride in having supplied
Frank's Bake Shop
with goods and services over the years

**Superior Paper Products Co.**
BANGOR, ME.
**Joseph Middleby Jr. Inc.**
BOSTON, MASS.
**S. Gumpert & Co.**
JERSEY CITY, N. J.
**Bangor Hydro-Electric Co.**
BANGOR, ME.
**Grant's Dairy Inc.**
BANGOR, ME.
**Citizens Utilities Co.**
BANGOR, ME.
**Arthur Chapin Co.**
BANGOR, ME.
**Berger Paper Co.**
LAWRENCE, MASS.
**Sherwin-Williams Co.**
BANGOR, ME.

# FRANK'S
## BAKE SHOP, INC.
*and CATERING SERVICE*
199 State St.    Tel. 3213 6710    Bangor, Maine

## COME IN TOMORROW AND MEET
### MR. JOHN RECHIS
#### Bakery Consultant, WESSON OIL CO.

John Rechis is known as one of the nation's top bakery specialists, having held demonstrations for commercial bakers all over the world. His talents come from 25 years of experience starting as a pan greaser and working up to master baker extraordinary.

While at Frank's Bake Shop Mr. Rechis will bake and serve New York Style Cheese Cake as well as a variety of cookies.

## COME IN . . . MEET MR. RECHIS THURSDAY
## FROM 1 P.M. TO 6 P.M.

**Facing page:** A full-page advertisement published in the Bangor Daily News on Wednesday, July 12, 1961 announced the "Grand Reopening" of the "Newly Remodeled, Sparkling Fresh Shop," an event slated for Thursday, July 13.

**Above:** To celebrate the grand reopening, Wesson Oil Co., a major supplier to Frank's Bake Shop, sent John Rechis to meet with customers and demonstrate the type of baking for which Frank's had been known since 1945. A bakery consultant with Wesson Oil, Rechis was a master baker who planned to cook and serve "New York Style Cheese Cake" and cookies to Frank's customers on July 13.

**Right:** The ad also showed that, after just 16 years in business, Frank's Bake Shop had earned a reputation as a reliable customer for many well-known local businesses.

The following firms take pride in having supplied

Frank's Bake Shop

with goods and services over the years

**Superior Paper Products Co.**
BANGOR, ME.

**Joseph Middleby Jr. Inc.**
BOSTON, MASS.

**S. Gumpert & Co.**
JERSEY CITY, N. J.

**Bangor Hydro-Electric Co.**
BANGOR, ME.

**Grant's Dairy Inc.**
BANGOR, ME.

**Citizens Utilities Co.**
BANGOR, ME.

**Arthur Chapin Co.**
BANGOR, ME.

**Berger Paper Co.**
LAWRENCE, MASS.

**Sherwin-Williams Co.**
BANGOR, ME.

Enjoying the brief moment of fame, Joe and Frank knew their bakery was better known for something else.

"The Soucy brothers say their chicken pot pie is more famous all over Maine than their catering to the appetites of the Hollywood crowd," the BDN reported.

The Soucys managed a multi-faceted business in the 1960s. "Uncle Frank did most of the cake decorating [and] Dad mostly took care of the bakery and the catering," said Bernadette Soucy Gaspar, Joe's oldest daughter. "Both helped each other when needed."

Joe also did a lot of baking and cooking in the bakery, Bernadette recalled.

Catering was a major focus throughout the '60s. According to Bernadette, Bangor lacked specific "event centers" then, and many functions happened in such places as the Bangor Auditorium, local church halls (popular for wedding receptions and family reunions),

The members of the bowling team sponsored by Frank's Bake Shop in the 1960s were (from left) Jim Soucy, Dick Baker, Don Pushaw, Ben Gunn, Don "Shoes" McCann (his nickname came from his very large feet), and Richard Joaquin.

Galen Cole (right) greets comedian Frank Fontaine (left) as he arrives to entertain the crowd arriving in Bangor to celebrate the 50th anniversary of Cole's Express. The Cole family retained Frank's Bake Shop to cater the celebration's meal, which featured prime rib, and Fontaine said that he'd never had prime rib as good as what he'd had from Frank's.

the Masonic Lodge on Main Street in Bangor, and elsewhere.

Frank's Bake Shop often provided everything associated with catering a meal: tables, chairs, food, table linen, plates and utensils, and, of course, the food. The Soucys catered some events on a regular basis—such as monthly meetings of Darling's Auto Parts—and other events that occurred only once in a lifetime.

One example of the latter was the 50th anniversary of Cole's Experience, celebrated by the Cole family in 1967. The headline entertainer for the event was Frank Fontaine, a comedian best known for his role as "Crazy Guggenheim" on TV's *The Jackie Gleason Show.*

"We served prime rib that evening," Bernadette said. "Frankie Fontaine came out to the serving area to shake the hand of the person who roasted the meat ... [He] said he had been all over the world and had not had prime rib as good as ours. So we say we made the best prime rib in the world!"

**Above:**
Dwight Fraser and Ethel Lizotte make pies at Frank's Bake Shop in the 1960s.

**Below:**
In February 1965, the catering staff at Frank's Bake Shop included (from left) Laura Murray, Joe Flanagan, and Lorraine Giles, a cousin of Joe Soucy.

**Above:** Since opening on Hancock Street in Bangor in October 1945, Frank's Bake Shop has baked many decorative (and delicious) cakes for such events as birthdays, wedding receptions, retirement parties, and anniversaries.

**Below:** When Frank's Bake Shop prepared a cake celebrating the 65th anniversary of St. John's Women's Council, a baker decorated the cake with a full-color (and edible) drawing of St. John's Catholic Church in Bangor.

People visiting the Roosevelt Cottage on Campobello Island today encounter lovely gardens and landscaping similar to the grounds surrounding the cottage during the June 1960 filming of *Sunrise at Campobello.* Frank's Bake Shop of Bangor catered meals for the cast and crew during filming; the event was among the highlights of the careers of Joe and Walteen Soucy.

# Chapter 5

# Sunrise at Campobello

Americans traveling to Campobello Island in the first 60 years of the 20th century had to arrange passage by boat to the Canadian island. No bridge yet spanned the narrows between Campobello's western shore and nearby Lubec in Maine, although a ferry did cross the Lubec Channel on a daily basis. The island's most famous American summer resident, Franklin Delano Roosevelt, had frequently stayed in the Roosevelt cottage earlier in the century; he had enjoyed sailing in local waters.

After writing the 1958 play *Sunrise at Campobello,* Dore Schary took that lack of land-based contact between Lubec and Campobello into consideration when he decided to produce a movie by the same title. Schary, who wrote the screenplay, retained Vincent J. Donehue to direct the film, which was partially filmed on Campobello Island.

The cast included Ralph Bellamy as FDR, Greer Garson as Eleanor Roosevelt, Hume Cronyn as FDR political advisor Louis Howe, and Tim Considine (soon to be of *My Three Sons* fame) as James Roosevelt, FDR's son. The cast and crew arrived on Campobello Island in early June 1960.

Meanwhile, Hollywood-based Schary Productions had contacted Joe Soucy and inquired if Frank's Bake Shop in Bangor could cater full meals for the 96 people to be involved with filming *Sunrise*

Photo by Brian Swartz

**Above:** Before he became the president of the United States, Franklin Delano Roosevelt often summered at this cottage on Campobello Island in New Brunswick. In early June 1960, a film crew arrived on the island to shoot scenes from *Sunrise on Campobello*, a movie starring Ralph Bellamy as Roosevelt and Greer Garson as his wife, Eleanor. Seeking a caterer to keep the cast and crew fed, Hollywood-based Schary Productions contacted Joe Soucy at Frank's Bake Shop in Bangor.

*at Campobello.* Frank's had expanded into catering in the 1950s. Never afraid of a challenge, even if the work meant traveling 130 miles to a foreign island and another time zone, Joe agreed to provide the meals and staff to keep actors and film crew alike well fed and happy.

Cast and crew started arriving in Eastport by train on June 7 after filming had wrapped up at Hyde Park in New York. All equipment went by highway to Lubec, then across the ferry to Campobello.

On the island, the Frank's Bake Shop crew prepared and served meals in the hall belonging to St. Anne's Church. Work took Joe Soucy and his staff elsewhere, however; on Monday, June 13, bus drivers started picking up cast and crew members at 5:30 a.m., with three additional bus runs scheduled over the next 45 minutes. Filming took place that day in Eastport—and Joe Soucy and the Frank's Bake Crew staff were there.

The buses started rolling at 5:45 a.m. on Tuesday, June 14 to transport the cast and crew to Welshpool on Campobello Island. Along came the Frank's staff and the equipment and food they had to provide.

A Frank's employee (possibly Joe Soucy himself) recorded what was needed to serve a picnic-style lunch one particular day. The list included two tables and their legs (transported separately, the latter were fastened to the tables upon arrival at the meal-serving site), fruit, water, iced tea, 233 sandwich boxes, 144 paper plates, 120 forks, coffee and sugar, potato salad, four jars of mustard, salad dressing, plastic spoons, 200 "cold" cups, and 150 "hot" cups."

Such were the logistics involved when Frank's Bake Shop crossed an international border to cater meals for a movie cast and crew. Joe and Walteen Soucy and their staff members (including Dwight and Lois Fraser, Richard and Robert Soucy, and Ray Welch) interacted daily with Bellamy, Cronyn, and Garson, and later drew accolades from Schary Productions for the bakery's ability to deliver

FDR at Campobello Island, June 16, 1933.

meals in weather ranging from fog to sunshine.

And Soucy family lore suggests that Greer Garson had never (according to her) tasted lobster until Joe Soucy introduced her to the delicacy.

**Right:** Holding a pipe, actor Hume Cronyn poses for the camera on Campobello Island in New Brunswick in early June 1960. He played the role of Louis Howe during the filming of the movie "Sunrise at Campobello"; Frank's Bakery of Bangor catered the meals for the cast and crew.

**Facing page top:** Vincent J. Donehue directed the filming of the movie *Sunrise at Campobello,* released in late September 1960. With the all-star cast and a film crew slated to film on Campobello Island in New Brunswick early that June, Frank's Bake Shop of Bangor was hired to cater the many meals served to several dozen people, including stars Ralph Bellamy (Franklin Delano Roosevelt), Greer Garson (Eleanor Roosevelt), and Hume Cronyn (Louis Howe). With cast and crew members dressed to stay warm on a foggy day at Campobello, Joe Soucy (far right) and Walteen Soucy (second from right) serve a hot meal. At left is actor Tim Considine of *My Three Sons* TV fame; in *Sunrise at Campobello,* he played the role of James Roosevelt, FDR's son.

**Facing page bottom:** At one meal, Joe Soucy serves a large boiled lobster to actress Greer Garson, who played the role of Eleanor Roosevelt.

**Below:** Among the employees of Frank's Bake Shop who catered meals for the cast and crew of *Sunrise at Campobello* in early June 1960 were (from left) Robert Soucy, Don Soucy, Walteen Soucy, Lois Fraser, Joe Soucy, Dwight Fraser, Richard Soucy, and Ray Welch.

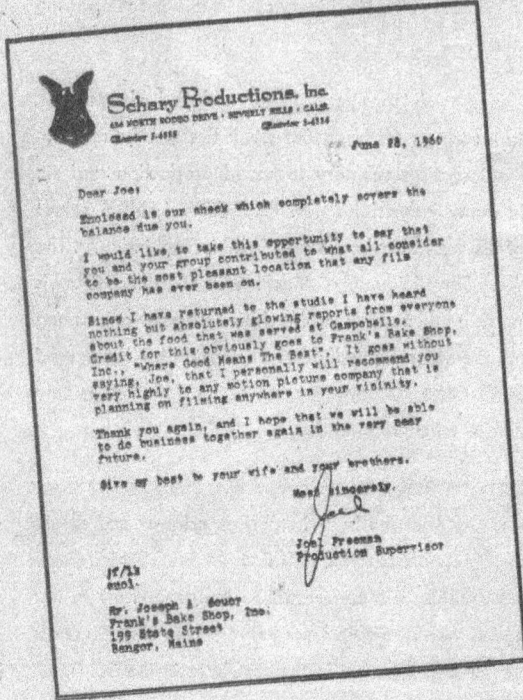

Soon after shooting for *Sunrise at Campobello* wrapped on Campobello Island in June 1960, Joe Soucy placed an ad in the Bangor Daily News reminding customers that Frank's Bakery could cater such typical events as banquets and weddings—and could also cater "to the STARS!"

Schary Productions, Inc.
434 NORTH RODEO DRIVE · BEVERLY HILLS · CALIF.
CRestview 5-4118          CRestview 5-4336

June 18, 1960

Dear Joe:

Enclosed is our check which completely covers the
balance due you.

I would like to take this opportunity to say that
you and your group contributed to what all consider
to be the most pleasant location that any film
company has ever been on.

Since I have returned to the studio I have heard
nothing but absolutely glowing reports from everyone
about the food that was served at Campobello.
Credit for this obviously goes to Frank's Bake Shop,
Inc., "Where Good Means The Best". It goes without
saying, Joe, that I personally will recommend you
very highly to any motion picture company that is
planning on filming anywhere in your vicinity.

Thank you again, and I hope that we will be able
to do business together again in the very near
future.

Give my best to your wife and your brothers.

Most sincerely,

Joel Freeman
Production Supervisor

jf/lk
encl.

Mr. Joseph A. Soucy
Frank's Bake Shop, Inc.
199 State Street
Bangor, Maine

Included in that ad was a letter to Joe Soucy by Joel Freeman, a production supervisor with Schary Productions, which had filmed *Sunrise at Campobello*. Freeman thanked Soucy for the excellent work that the Frank's staff had done in catering meals for the movie's cast and crew on Campobello Island.

Dwight Fraser, who worked 41 years at Frank's Bake Shop in Bangor, operates a commercial dough mixer inside the bakery in the 1970s.

# Chapter 6

# The 1970s:
# The Turkeys of
# Christmas Eve

Although most customers associated Frank's Bake Shop with the delicious foods sold at 199 State Street in Bangor, off-site catering remained a major business activity for the Soucys in the 1970s.

"We did many off-premises catering," recalled Bernadette Soucy Gaspar. Catered events included the installation of the Anah Shrine potentate, held each January in Bangor; the summer sailing season's kick-off held the Saturday of each Memorial Day weekend at the Bucks Harbor Yacht Club in Brooksville; and events held at the Masonic Lodge in Bangor.

"We did many champagne weddings on the coast," Bernadette said, including at places like Blue Hill. Frank's Bake Shop also catered events for The Jackson Lab and cocktail parties for the Schieffelins, a New York family that summered in Gouldsboro. Schieffelin & Company imported and distributed spirits and wines.

According to Bernadette, the Soucys adapted their catering services to reflect changing trends. Reception fare shifted from the finger foods popular in the 1960s to sit-down meals—dinner, a buffet, or full service—in the 1970s. That trend continued into the 1980s.

**Above:** Keeping busy preparing pastries and pies at Frank Bake Shop in the 1970s are Walter Beaulieu (left) and Dwight Fraser.

**Facing page:** A young visitor at Frank's Bake Shop watches Ben Gunn fill éclairs in the 1970s.

**Below:** Watched by that same young visitor, Tracy Porter rolls out dough at Frank's Bake Shop in the 1970s.

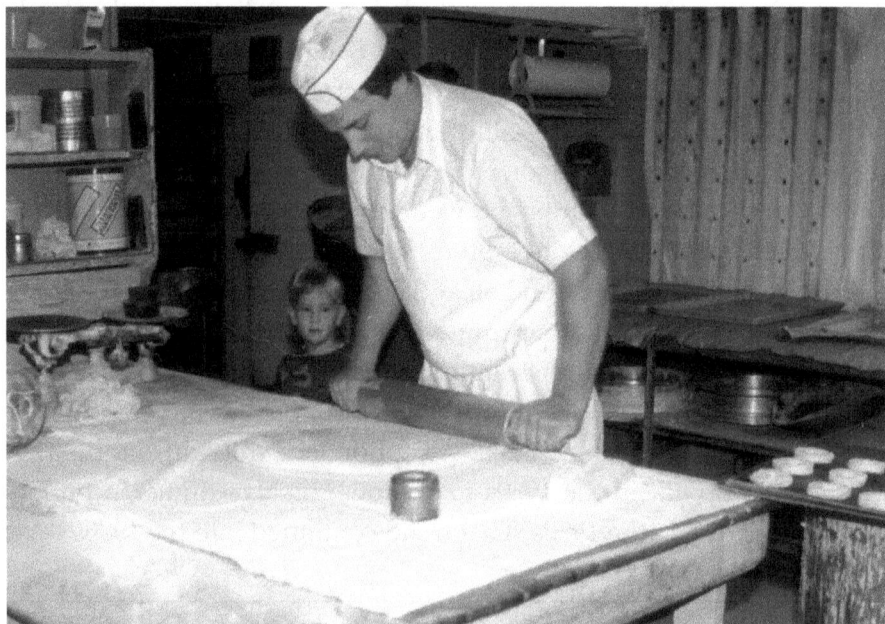

As he had done for many years, Joe Soucy opened the bakery for half days on Thanksgiving and Christmas to that customers who had purchased holidays meals could pick them up on the particular holiday. Joe prepared roast turkey, stuffing, and giblet gravy for these meals, which were popular; one Christmas Eve he roasted 36 turkeys.

"Every hour he would get up out of bed and go in and baste the turkeys," Bernadette said. When Joe sat down for the family's Christmas dinner, he dozed off.

Today customers can pick up their meals the day prior to Thanksgiving and Christmas, and Frank's Bake Shop is closed both holidays.

The period from the late 1960s to the late 1970s saw the children

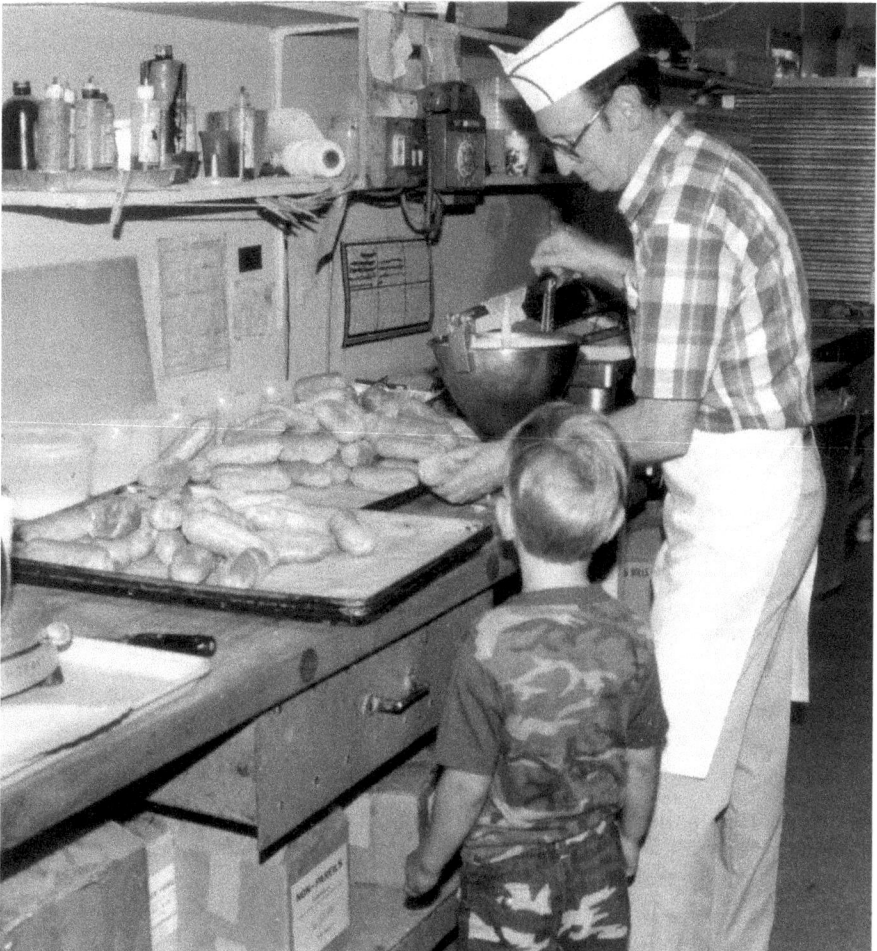

of Joe and Walteen Soucy—Joey, Bernadette, Richard, Theresa, and Fleurette—leaving home to pursue their own careers. All five were married between 1968 and 1972, and there was a lot of wedding planning. "We kept Mom busy," Bernadette said.

The greater Bangor region was changing as more people moved to the towns surrounding Bangor and Brewer. Interstate 95 now linked Bangor with towns to the north and west and made possible the development of the Bangor Mall; downtown Bangor was emerging from urban renewal, and many people thought that in-town businesses would suffer declines as shoppers shifted to the mall and other shopping centers that were sprouting up in the region.

But I-95 made such popular destinations as Frank's Bake Shop more accessible, especially to those people traveling across the Penobscot River from Brewer and then heading up State Street toward the mall. Business increased as more people discovered the tasty delights available at Frank's Bake Shop. And for shoppers wrapping up their shopping trips in Bangor, Frank's became an important stop on the way home to pick up chicken and turkey pies, pastries, sandwiches, and desserts to serve with the evening meal.

Sometime during the 1970s, Walter Beaulieu operates the new oven that was installed at Frank's Bake Shop in 1961. The oven remains in use today.

**Above:** Joe Flanagan (left) and Charlie Miller prepare pastries at Frank's Bake Shop in the 1970s.

**Below:** Keeping busy baking pastries and pies at Frank's Bake Shop in the 1970s are (from left) Tracy Porter, Walter Beaulieu, and Joe Flanagan.

**Above:** Joe Soucy visits with his niece, Jeanette Flora, and her son, John, outside Frank's Bake Shop at 199 State Street, Bangor in the 1970s.

**Facing page:** Along with his brother Joe, Frank Soucy Jr. was a co-owner of Frank's Bake Shop for many years. He and his wife, Mary Leen Soucy, were married for 55 years. During that time, Mary worked as the bookkeeper. The couple had three children—Frank III, Dianne, and Mary Elizabeth—who all worked at the bakery and on catering jobs while growing up.

**Below:** Frosting drizzles over freshly baked cinnamon rolls at Frank's Bake Shop. This particular pastry has been popular with the bakery's customers for several decades.

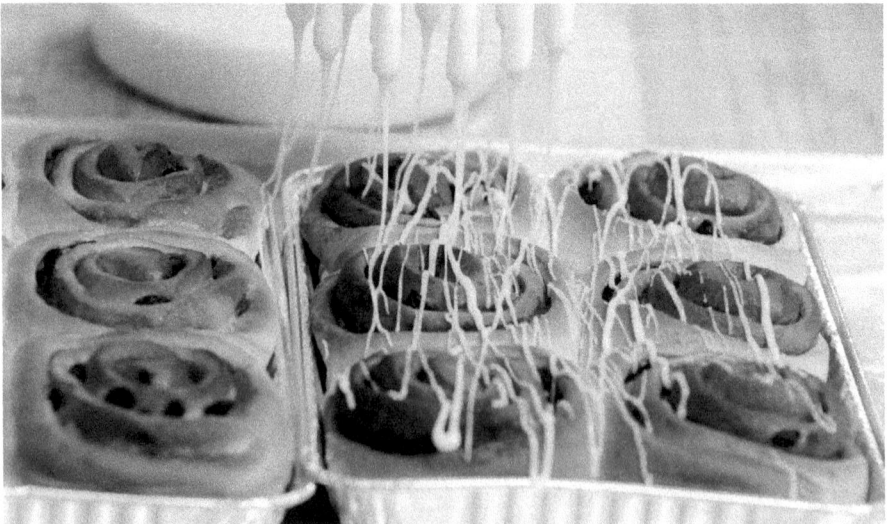

Bangor Daily News photo by Kevin Bennett

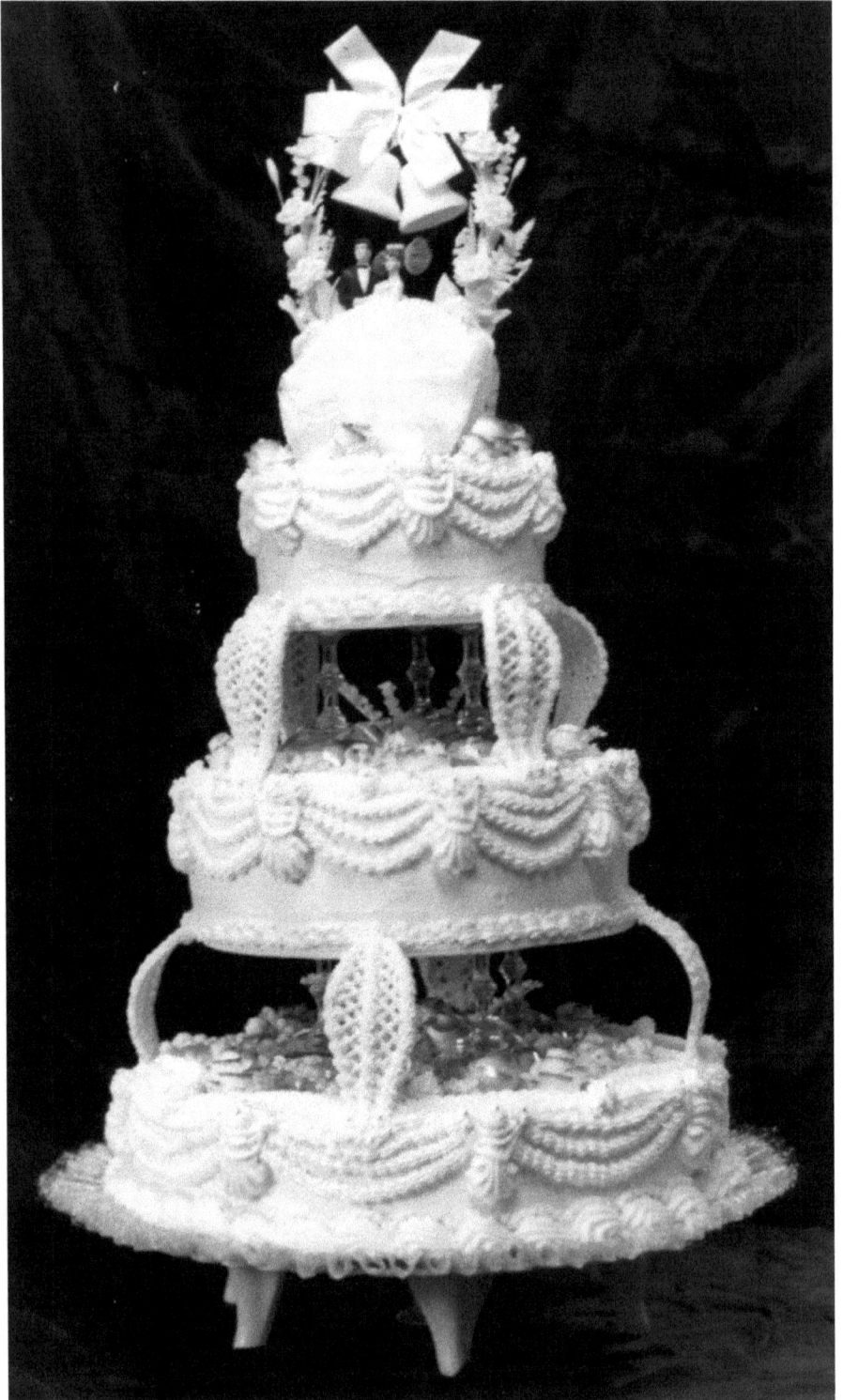

An exquisite wedding cake made by Frank Soucy Jr. in 1983.

# Chapter 7

# The 1980s:
# Friendly Faces Greet
# Customers at Frank's

The 1980s brought change to Frank's Bake Shop as evolving retail trends introduced larger (and competing) bakeries to Bangor. But Frank's bested the competition as the third generation of Soucys helped manage the bakery.

According to Bernadette Soucy Gaspar, the "big-box stores" arriving in Bangor featured large baked-goods sections. Several smaller grocery stores consolidated into a few massive (by Bangor-area standards) supermarkets, each with on-site bakeries and products similar to those carried by existing smaller bakeries.

Just as the expanding outreach of the Bangor Mall was predicted to devastate downtown stores, so were the large retail bakery outlets expected to draw too many customers from smaller bakeries to leave the latter economically viable.

Both predictions were wrong. Retail shopping now thrives downtown, and customers continued to flock to Frank's Bake Shop because of its fresh foods and friendly staff. In fact, customers found even more reasons why Frank's was the best bakery to visit in Bangor.

Consider parking: After navigating expansive parking lots and

Walteen and Joseph Soucy celebrated their 40th wedding anniversary in 1983.

walking long distances to reach big-box stores, customers realized they could park on Brown or State streets, right next to Frank's Bake Shop, and walk just a short distance. That was important in cold weather.

Consider the staff: Customers coming in the front door at Frank's encountered familiar faces. Some employees had worked many years in the bakery, and the Soucys—Joe and Walteen and Frank and some of their adult children—were usually there, sometimes in the production area, sometimes at the counter. The Soucys and their staff often knew customers by name and greeted them accordingly.

Consider the freshness of the foods: Employees started the day's baking at Frank's Bake Shop early each morning, and customers knew they were buying doughnuts and other pastries fresh out of the oven. The chicken and turkey pies became mealtime favorites as busy families had less time to cook at home.

All these factors (and others) made shopping at Frank's Bake Shop a positive experience for area residents — and still do.

Joe and Walteen Soucy celebrated their 40th wedding anniversary during a surprise party held in 1983; they started spending winters in Florida about the same time, staying in New Smyrna Beach. "Dad took his apron off in October and put it back on in May," said Bernadette.

**Below:** In 1983, the landscaped grounds at Frank's Bake Shop attracted the admiration of (from left) Joe Soucy, Andrew Dow, Gordon Dow (holding his daughter, Amy), and Theresa Soucy. The gardens were created by Walteen Soucy.

**Above:**
A favorite pastime of Walteen Soucy was landscaping the grounds around Frank's Bake Shop, located at 199 State Street in Bangor. In the mid-1980s, she and her husband, Joe Soucy, pose by some of her handiwork behind the bakery.

**Below:**
Frank's famous éclairs, which the bakery has made for decades.

Joseph Soucy stands amidst the construction activity involving a major remodeling of Frank's Bake Shop in the 1980s. The Soucys have remodeled the bakery several times since moving it to 199 State Street in Bangor in October 1947.

Joe Soucy watches as construction workers renovate a portion of Frank's Bake Shop in the 1980s. Joe's son, Dick Soucy, was among the people involved in this particular project.

Three construction workers put the finishing touches on part of a major renovation project undertaken at Frank's Bake Shop in the 1980s.

Sometimes a renovation project at Frank's Bake Shop requires a construction worker to become acquainted with the inside of the baking equipment, as one worker (right) did during a major renovation project in the 1980s.

**Above:** Among the employees of Frank's Bake Shop in February 1981 are (from left) Dick Doll, Arlene Oldheine, Walter Beaulieu, unidentified, Ben Gunn, and Dwight Fraser.

**Below:** In the 1980s, Walteen Soucy of Frank's Bake Shop shares a smile with Sister Mary Norberta of St. Joseph Hospital.

**Above:**
Taking a brief break while working at Frank's Bake Shop in 1985, (from left) Walter Beaulieu, Ben Gunn, Joseph Soucy, Frank Soucy, and Dwight Frasier pose with a pan of raised glazed donuts, a cake, and turkey pies.

**Left:**
Another beautiful wedding cake made by Frank Soucy Jr. in 1983.

**Above:** Joe Soucy chats with his daughter, Theresa Soucy, outside Frank's Bake Shop in the 1980s.

**Below:** The sign below was in place by the 1990s, and hung over Frank's Bake Shop for decades.

Joe Soucy stands at the rear entrance to the Soucy family home at 199 State Street, Bangor on August 30, 1987. As they had for several years, Joe and his wife, Walteen, would head for Florida in a few months and spend the winter there.

**Above:** An employee of Lynch Construction uses an excavator to remove dirt behind Frank's Bake Shop in 1993. The work was part of a major construction project to connect the bakery (right) with an adjacent wood-frame building that is now home to Healthy Solutions, another business owned by the Soucy family.

**Below:** His tape measure on his belt, Dick Soucy stands inside the main entrance of Frank's Bake Shop during a 1994 remodeling project. Dick, who has supervised several such projects over the years, installed the two entrance doors behind him.

# Chapter 8

# The 1990s: Raspberry Tarts Top the Chart

**W**hen Joe Soucy died at age 74 on December 11, 1991, he left behind a close-knit family, memories of his infectious smile, and a bakery that was poised to grow.

"He was a most generous, remarkable, gentle, and giving man," daughter Theresa Soucy recalled in 1994. "Everyone loved him. No friend would ever leave his house without an armload of cookies, cakes, and bread to take home.

"His spirit was overflowing, and no one ever saw him without a smile," Theresa said.

The Soucys had acquired a building adjacent to their State Street bakery some years earlier and had operated other businesses there. In 1993, Joe's five children decided to connect the two buildings, a project for which Dick Soucy served as the general contractor. He has handled similar projects and performed routine maintenance at the bakery for many years. He worked with the various subcontractors to ensure that the construction project was completed on time and within budget. The project required some serious earthwork and construction.

"We literally had our house put on steel beams in order to dig

**Above:**
Located across from Miller Drug, Frank's Bake Shop (lower right) stretches for three-quarters of the State Street block between Boyd and Brown streets. As seen in this June 1999 aerial photo, the bakery is located in the heart of Bangor's traditional East Side.

**Below:**
The image below, cropped and blown up from the aerial shot above, offers more detail of Frank's Bake Shop at 199 State Street in Bangor.

During a remodeling project being undertaken at Frank's Bake Shop in September 1998, Theresa Soucy (left) and Lorraine Catell take a brief break amidst the hubbub.

the cellar down three feet in order to even it off with the level of the bakery cellar," Bernadette Soucy Gaspar said.

By now Frank's Bake Shop occupied the entire first floor of 199 State Street. The bakery's entrance was located where the Soucys had once entered their home, which was in the same building.

By expanding their retail space the full width of the building at 199 State Street, the Soucys were able to add some chairs and tables where customers could sit and enjoy their morning coffee and pastries. The display cases expanded, too, and a particularly seasonal pastry received special attention.

"We started making tarts," Bernadette explained, as strawberries, raspberries, and blueberries came into season each year. "The first year it was advertised in the Bangor Daily News, we sold out."

Because she was so involved in making the tarts, customers dubbed Bernadette the "Tart Queen." In a few years a local TV station crew interviewed her about the fresh (and delicious) tarts; the next morning, Frank's had far more customers looking for tarts than expected!

"Between the strawberry, raspberry, and blueberry tarts, we usually sell about 5,000 to 6,000 a year," Bernadette said. "We have made as many as 8,300 tarts in a summer.

But it's the raspberry tarts that customers really want.

"Raspberry is the top seller by two to three times over the other kinds combined," she said.

The 1990s saw "event centers" open in the Bangor area and offer catering services for events held on site. Frank's Bake Shop's catering changed more to preparing the food, which a customer could either pick up or the shop could deliver to an event site. Frank's could also deliver the food and set up the equipment and pick it up later.

Theresa Soucy represents Frank's Bake Shop Catering Services during a 1995 bridal show held at the Bangor Civic Center.

**Above:**
Barbara Simpson, who was a cake decorator at Frank's Bake Shop for many years, decorated this wedding cake in the 1990s.

**Below:**
Working at Frank's in the 1990s are Betty Spinney (left) and Shirley Dyer.

A Halloween celebration held at Frank's Bake Shop in the 1990s saw Bernadette (left) and Sue Mallett dressed as bobby-soxers.

**Above:** Participating in the same Halloween celebration at Frank's Bake Shop in the 1990s were employees Ethel Tuck (left), dressed as a clown, and Julie Bartlett, dressed as a football.

**Below:** In 1994, Theresa Soucy and Dick Soucy (first and second from left) work on the façade of the bakery during renovations with Rick Duplisea (right).

The bakery began making tarts in the 1990s. They were an instant hit, and the bakery is well known for them today. Pictured above are strawberry tarts; at right is a blueberry tart. But their raspberry tarts (below) are in the most demand, outselling all others combined.

The five siblings posed for this photo in front of the bakery in 1995. From left are Joseph Soucy, Theresa Soucy, Bernadette Soucy Gaspar, Fleurette Soucy Dow, and Dick Soucy.

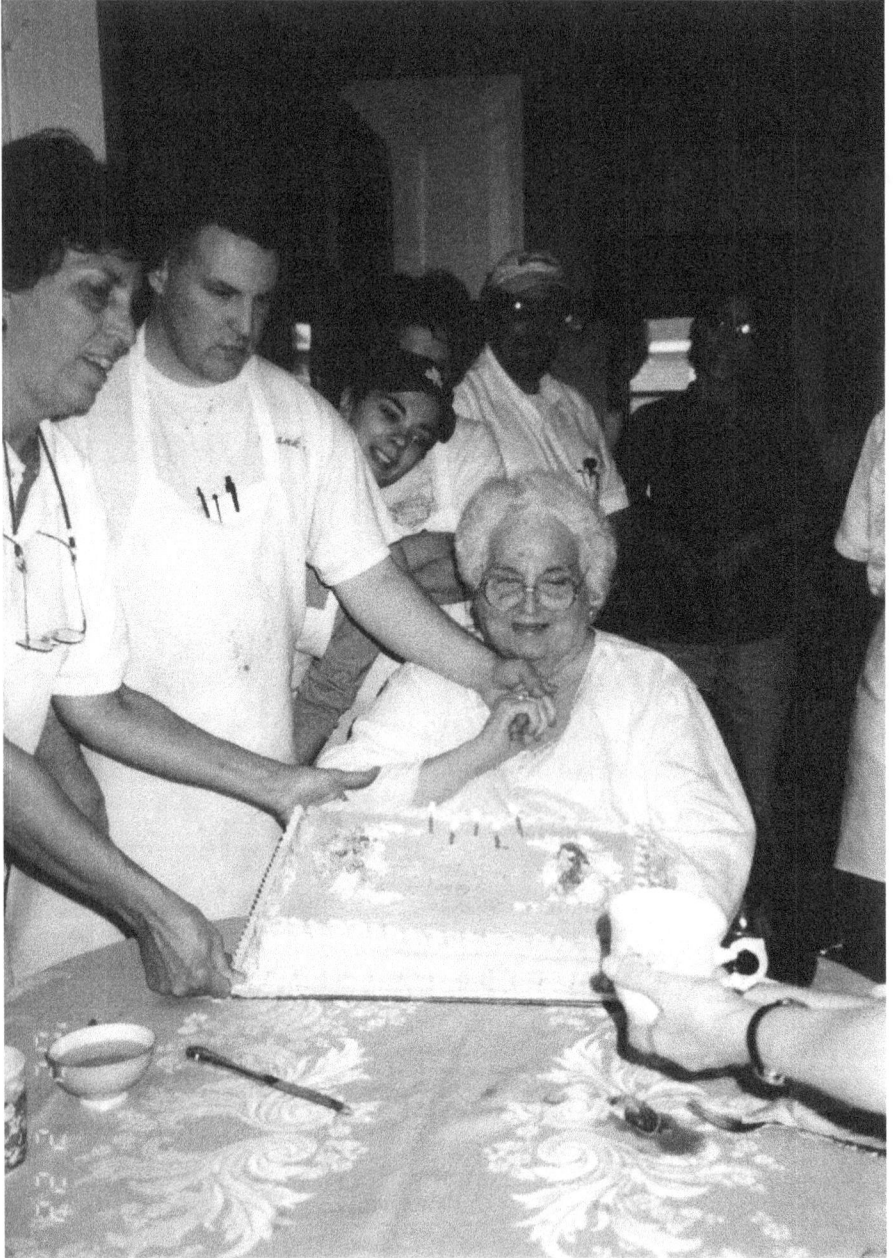

On February 22, 2002, friends and relatives celebrated the 86th birthday of Walteen Soucy. Among the people attending the party were (standing, from left) Bernadette Soucy Gaspar, Jaye Gross, Heather Riley, Melanie Sites, Joe Pray, and Lois Dennis.

# Chapter 9

# The 21st Century

**A** new century brought a generational transition to Frank's Bake Shop. Family and friends gathered in Bangor on February 22, 2002 to help family matriarch Walteen Soucy celebrate her 86th birthday. She fortuitously shared February 22 with George Washington, and for many years she enjoyed the fact that her birthday coincided with a national holiday.

"Since Mom was born on Washington's birthday, her parents wanted to give her a name starting with a W," said Bernadette Soucy Gaspar. "So they called her Waltereen, but she didn't like it, so it was shortened to Walteen," and sometimes "she was called Walt or Teen!"

After Joe Soucy had died in 1991, the ownership of Frank's Bake Shop shifted to Walteen and the Soucys' five children: Joey, Bernadette, Dick, Theresa, and Fleurette. Maintaining the tradition that she and Joe had started, Walteen continued spending her winters in Florida until 1997.

Walteen passed away on December 9, 2002, and the third generation of the Soucy family assumed full management of Frank's Bake Shop. Joey and Fleurette live with their families in Massachusetts and New Hampshire respectively; Bernadette and Theresa work full time at the bakery, and when not teaching physical education at John Bapst Memorial High School, Dick often joins his sisters at the family-run business. He also maintains the bakery and other

The Soucy family celebrated the 60th anniversary of Frank's Bake Shop in 2005.

properties owned by the Soucys.

The 60th anniversary festivities in 2005 received extensive coverage in the local media, and Frank Soucy Jr. shared some memories with reporters. Earlier that year, a California couple had expressed to him their pleasure in finding Frank's Bake Shop still located at 199 State Street; the bakery had baked their wedding cake many years ago, the couple explained, and they planned to have their 50th-anniversary cake baked at Frank's, too.

After working for 65 years at the bakery, Frank Soucy Jr. retired in 2010; he died in January 2012.

Today, the buildings encompassing Frank's Bake Shop and other Soucy-family-owned businesses stretch along three-quarters of the State Street block between Boyd and Brown streets. Beside the bakery is Healthy Solutions, which the Soucys opened some years ago.

Celebrating its 70th anniversary in October 2015, Frank's Bake Shop is well known across Maine—and wherever former Bangor residents move throughout the United States, they take memories of Frank's with them.

And customers remember Frank's for more than its delicious pastries and homemade, ready-to-go meals. Theresa Soucy explained what is special about Frank's some years ago; her words

**Right:** Taking a moment to relax during a busy day at Frank's Bake Shop sometime during the 2000s are (from left) Theresa Soucy, cousin Paul McCann, and Bernadette.

**Below:** Paul McCann squirts the dough for tea-sized puff shells onto a pan at Frank's Bake Shop sometime during the 2000s.

apply today.

"When people come into Frank's, we always try to make the customer feel like a friend," Theresa said. "We provide one-on-one service to our customers; we're part of their families.

"At Frank's, we stress quality," Theresa said. "We want to know that the person who walks in our shop leaves with a smile. People love coming into our little bakery. We will continue to uphold our motto" …

… which is "Where GOOD means the BEST."

For the past 70 years, Frank's Bake Shop and the Soucy family have certainly done so—and will continue to do so for years to come.

**Facing page:** Theresa Soucy stirs topping into freshly made ice cream at Frank's Bake Shop on Tuesday, May 11, 2004.

**Below:** The Soucy family held a 60th anniversary celebration of Frank's Bake Shop on Monday, October 17, 2005. During the afternoon, Theresa Soucy (right) talks with Joan Osler of Dedham (left) and her daughter Kate of Bangor while waiting for their lunches, which were being prepared by the bakery's staff.

Bangor Daily News photo by Denise Farwell

Bangor Daily News Photo by Megan Rathfon

Bangor Daily News photos by John Clarke Russ

**Top:** Frank's Bake Shop clerk Ethel Tuck gives change to customer Jim Wheelden of Orrington December 21, 2005. Wheelden had purchased bread rolls for a family holiday gathering. The days immediately prior to Christmas are extremely busy at Frank's as the staff bakes additional holiday delicacies.

**Above:** The kitchen at Frank's Bake Shop is a busy place just before Christmas 2005 as Theresa Soucy helps Aimee Humphrey (left) and Aaron Hayden prepare apple pies.

Bangor Daily News photo by Gabor Degre

**Above:**
Susan Overlock decorates heart-shaped cookies at Frank's Bake Shop in early December 2007.

**Left:**
Gingerbread cookies are a popular holiday treat prepared each Christmas season at Frank's Bake Shop.

Bangor Daily News photo by John Clarke Russ

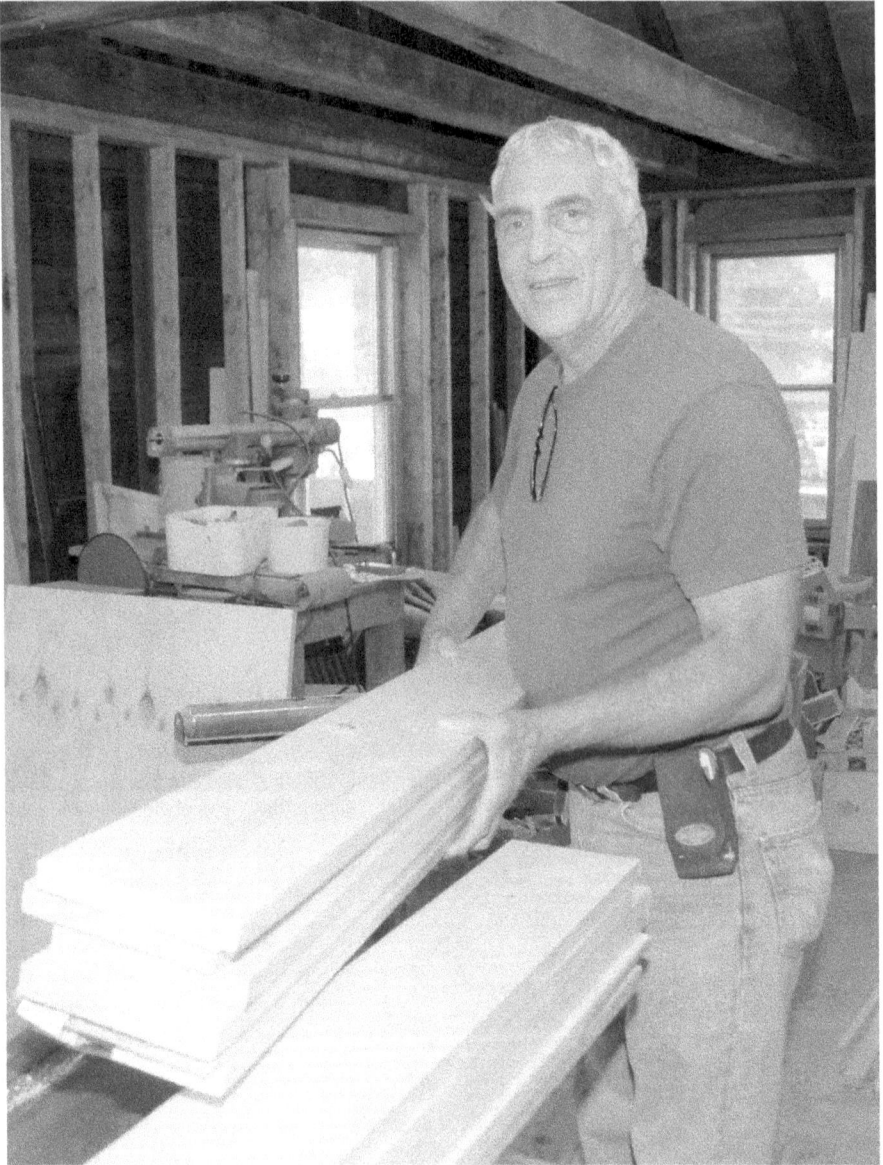

Photo by Brian Swartz

Since he was young, Dick Soucy has worked on many remodeling projects for his family's business, Frank's Bake Shop. He has also served as the general contractor for several bakery-related projects, including a 1993 expansion that connected the bakery with the adjacent building in which the Soucy family-owned Healthy Solutions is now located.

**Above:** Many members of the Frank's Bake Shop family gathered in the mid-2000s to honor Ethel Tuck (center) upon her retirement after 11 years of service. Leaning against the counter are Michael Hunt (left) and Theresa Soucy, next to Ethel Tuck. Behind the counter are (from left) unidentified, Madeline Margraf, Lorien Wood, Melanie Sites, Christopher Hood, Roxi Lerbeck (behind Tuck), Bernadette Soucy Gaspar, Jenna Tidd, Julie Bartlett, Karen Walker, Sue Mallett, Cindy Fowle, Teresa Duplisea, and Gailene Friedly.

**Right:** On her final day of work at Frank's Bake Shop, Ethel Tuck displays the cake that was prepared for her by the bakery's staff. Ethel, who had worked 11 years at the bakery, was affectionately known as "Auntie."

Bangor Daily News photo by Bridget Brown

**Above:** Responding to customer requests, Frank's Bake Shop introduced gluten-free products early in the 21st century. Bernadette displays several gluten-free delicacies at the bakery on Friday, August 6, 2010.

**Below:** Sharing a smile at the main entrance to Frank's Bake Shop are sisters Theresa Soucy (left) and Bernadette, who have worked together at the bakery for many years.

**Below:** A cousin of the Soucy family, Paul McCann prepares cake batter at Frank's Bake Shop in mid-October 2010. McCann had operated Paul's Pastries in Brewer for many years, but after retiring, he joined the staff at Frank's.

**Bottom:** Susan Overlock decorates a wedding cake at Frank's Bake Shop in mid-October 2010.

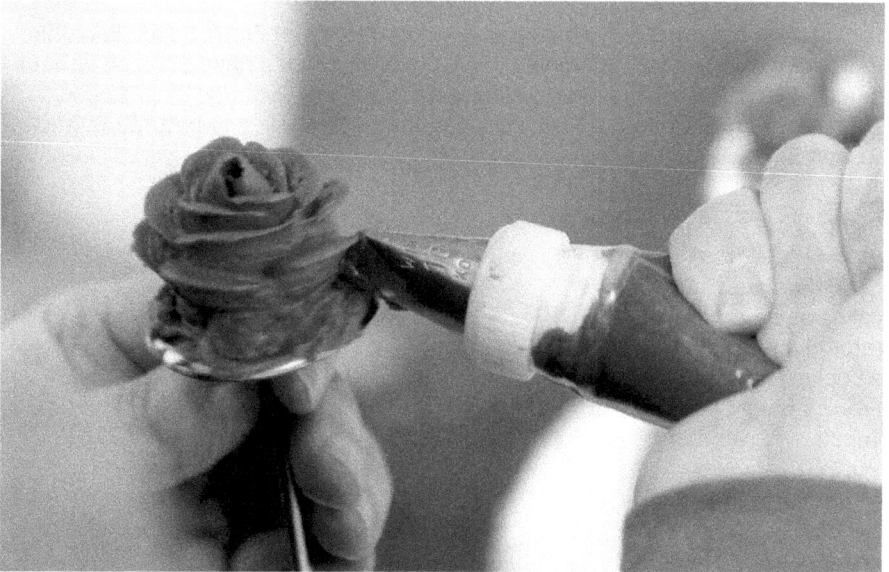

Bangor Daily News photos by Linda Coan O'Kresik

Bangor Daily News photo by Gabor Degre

**Above:** Cookies and cakes decorated for the holiday season are displayed at Frank's Bake Shop a few weeks prior to Christmas 2007.

**Facing page top:** After helping his father and brother launch Frank's Bake Shop in 1945 and working there for the next 65 years, Frank Soucy Jr. decided to retire in autumn 2010. He relaxes at the bakery that October 13.

**Facing page bottom:** Family members gathered to honor Frank Soucy Jr. on his retirement during a reception held in his honor at Frank's Bake Shop on November 13, 2010. Among those attending were (from left) Richard "Dick" Soucy, Theresa Soucy, Bernadette Soucy Gaspar, Frank Soucy Jr., Fleurette Dow, and Joseph Soucy.

**Right:** Thanksgiving turkeys peer from hand-decorated cupcakes as a cake decorator plucks one from a cookie sheet at Frank's Bake Shop on Tuesday, November 26, 2013.

Bangor Daily News photo by Kevin Bennett

Bangor Daily News photos by Linda Coan O'Kresik

**Above:** The fifth generation of the Soucy family tries his hand at stirring the pot at Frank's Bake Shop, circa 2003. One-year-old Finn, the great-great grandson of Frank Soucy Sr., is all smiles because he has figured out that the pastry he is making is delicious!

**Facing page, top:** The beginning of Maine's wild blueberry harvest finds Bernadette Soucy Gaspar (left) and Theresa Soucy making fresh blueberry tarts. The bakery also makes raspberry and strawberry tarts when those fruits are in season.

**Facing page, bottom:** While Bernadette scoops fresh wild Maine blueberries into a tart shell (left), Theresa decorates each tart with the special whipped cream that helps enhance the pastry's flavor.

**Top:** One Halloween celebration in the 2000s saw the employees of Frank's Bake Shop dress up as various characters. Among those participating were (from left) Bernadette Soucy Gaspar, Gailene Friedly, Melanie Sites, Roxi Lerbeck (sitting), Karen Walker, Theresa Soucy, Julie Bartlett, Madeline Margraf, Chelsea Kenney, and Alicia Bissell.

**Above:** Another Halloween celebration in the 2000s saw these employees of Frank's Bake Shop creating some unusual costumes: (from left) Jenna Tidd, Julie Bartlett, Lorien Wood, Karen Walker, Gailene Friedly, Roxi Lerbeck, and Theresa Soucy.

Bangor Daily News photo by Kevin Bennett

The countdown to Thanksgiving is on as Julie Bartlett (right) and Theresa Soucy remove fresh baked pies from the oven at Frank's Bake Shop on Tuesday, November 26, 2013.

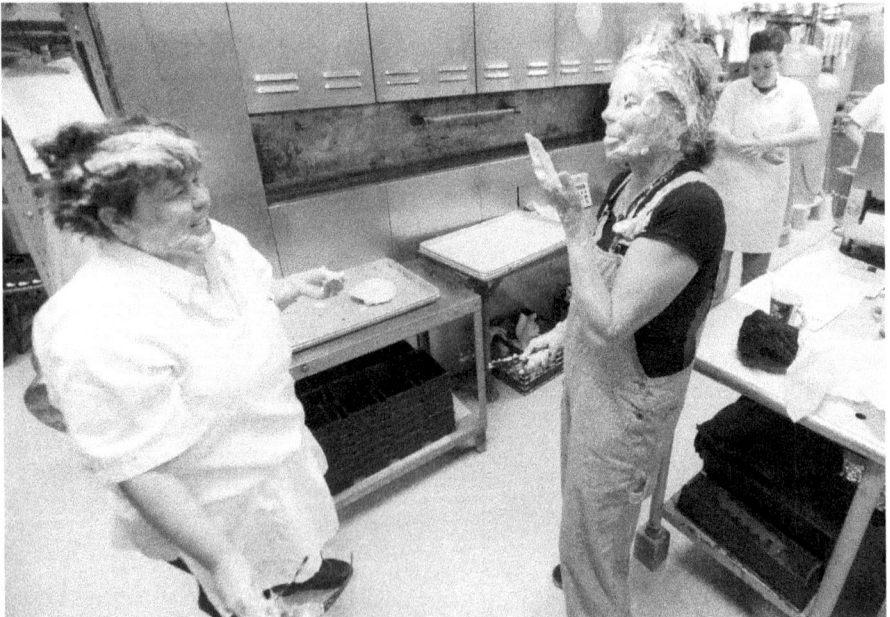

Bangor Daily News photos by Kevin Bennett

**Top:** With Thanksgiving just two days away, baker Kelly Proulx (left) carries a tray of coconut cream pies to be boxed at Frank's Bake Shop on November 26, 2013.

**Above:** Julie Bartlett (left) and Theresa Soucy share a good laugh and start cleaning up after they eased the pre-Thanksgiving pressure at Frank's Bake Shop with a pie fight on Tuesday, November 26, 2013.

**Below:** Seamus Lowell folds pie boxes at Frank's Bake Shop on Tuesday, November 26, 2013. Customers had already ordered more than 600 fresh pies for serving at Thanksgiving only two days hence.

**Bottom:** With hundreds of Thanksgiving pies on order, Jane Heath checks the pie inventory at Frank's Bake Shop on Tuesday, November 26, 2013. The bakery's employees made and baked more than 600 pies for customers.

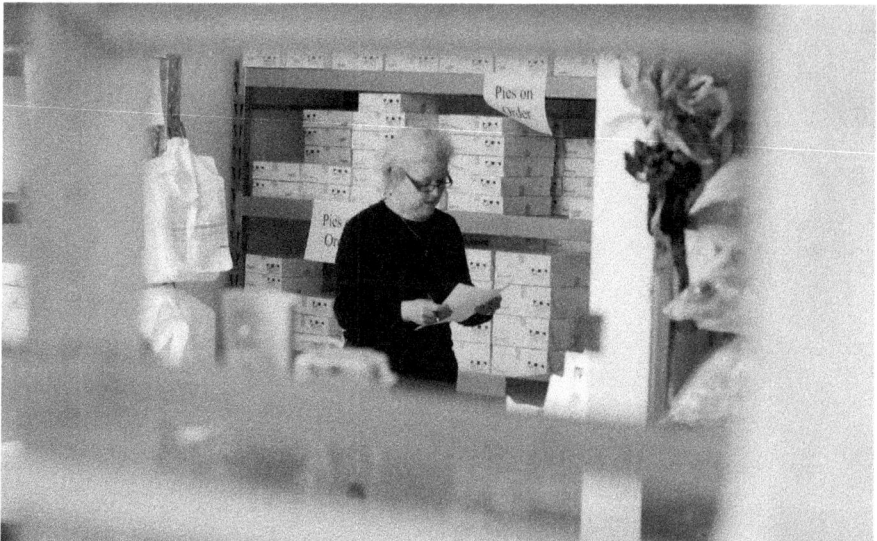

Bangor Daily News photos by Kevin Bennett

**Above:**
The third-generation owners of Frank's Bake Shop are (from left) Theresa Soucy, Richard "Dick" Soucy, Bernadette Soucy Gaspar, Fleurette Dow, and Joseph Soucy.

**Facing page top:**
The logo for the 70th anniversary of Frank's Bake Shop.

**Facing page bottom:**
A close-up of the three men who started it all: Joseph Soucy, Frank Soucy Sr., and Frank Soucy Jr.

ANNIVERSARY
70th
FRANK'S
1945          2015
"Where GOOD Means the BEST"

# About the Author

**B**rian F. Swartz worked initially as a reporter and then as an editor for 27 years at the Bangor Daily News, where his work introduced him to the people and places that make Maine such a great place to live. Also a professional photographer, he now writes for various Maine-based newspapers and magazines.

Swartz authored and photo-illustrated *An American Homecoming,* which details the "welcome home" extended by Maine residents to American military personnel returning from the 1992 Gulf War. In collaboration with Richard R. Shaw, he co-authored the recently published *Legendary Locals of Bangor,* highlighting 115 people who played roles in the history of Bangor.

A Civil War historian, Swartz writes *Maine at War,* a column about the roles that Mainers played in that conflict; weekly columns are posted at maineatwar.bangordailynews.com. He also lectures about Maine and the Civil War.

Swartz lives in central Maine with his wife Susan and their fluffy orange cat. Active in a local church, he enjoys sharing adventures with his grandchildren and friends and exploring the United States with Susan.